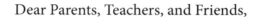

Dear Parents, Teachers, and Friends,

In early 2018, I was inspired to write a children's book after an experience I shared with my 4-year-old daughter, Autumn. One weekend, Autumn watched me straighten and style my long, natural hair and told me she wanted "princess hair" like mine. Immediately, as a mother to a little black girl, I felt compelled to be Autumn's mirror, and I knew it was time for a change.

Hair Like Me is simply a children's story about a little girl who learns the true beauty of princess hair.

It's time to celebrate one another's beautiful, physical differences. True beauty is not measured by mainstream media's limited beauty standards imposed on society through a handful of images. Beauty is diverse and anyone can wear a crown! And children, especially black children who are underrepresented or misrepresented in media, will know this more and more when they see themselves in a variety of imagery.

Parents! We face tough decisions while raising our children, and often, our choices are much more impactful than the words we speak. I want to empower parents who walk the line between teaching and setting an example for their children. Parenting is not easy and there will be tough choices. I'm here to encourage us to continue BEING the example as much as possible. We won't get it right every single time, but as long as we know they're watching, we have to keep trying!

Lastly, this story is a reminder to women and girls everywhere that loving their hair is important, but beauty and confidence emanates from within.

Love,
Heather

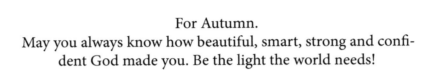

For Autumn.
May you always know how beautiful, smart, strong and confident God made you. Be the light the world needs!

Love always,
Mommy

Hair Like Me

HEATHER BURRIS

illustrated by
ARIEL MENDEZ

Autumn loves to imitate Mommy.

Autumn wears sneakers just like Mommy.

Autumn talks on her cell phone just like Mommy.

Autumn even bakes just like Mommy.

Autumn and Mommy do everything together!

One evening before bed,
Autumn was watching
Mommy wash and style her
hair.

She noticed how Mommy's naturally curly hair became straight.

When Mommy was finished, Autumn said to her, "You look beautiful, Mommy! Just like a princess!"
"Thank you, sweetheart," Mommy said.

"I want princess hair like yours!" Autumn exclaimed.
Then she pretended to style her hair just like Mommy had done.

"But Autumn, your hair is beautiful! I love your hair!
Now it's time for bed!" Mommy helped Autumn change into
her pajamas and settle into bed.

Autumn was sad. She wanted princess hair like Mommy.

As she drifted off to sleep, Autumn imagined herself with hair that could be tied up into a beautiful scarf like Mommy's.

Mommy lie awake that night. She thought long and hard about
what Autumn had said about "princess hair".

When Mommy was a little girl, she wanted princess hair too! But her hair was like Autumn's.

Growing up in school, many of her friends did not have hair like hers.

Mommy tried everything she could to have princess hair.

Mommy tried to wear her hair up.
Mommy tried to wear her hair down.

Mommy even tried to wear fake hair.
But nothing had worked!

She knew how Autumn felt all too well. That feeling of being
different because of her hair.

Mommy had learned to love her hair as she got older. But she knew that if she kept her hair styled long and straight, Autumn would think this was princess hair, and start to dislike her own hair.

Mommy felt that it was her job to teach Autumn that she was beautiful inside and out, and that princess hair is beautiful hair, no matter the style.

Mommy loved Autumn so much that she wanted Autumn to love everything about herself, too! Mommy knew what she had to do.

The next day, while Autumn
was away at school, Mommy
went to the hair salon.

"How do you want your hair styled today?" The stylist asked. Immediately, Mommy responded, "I want you to cut it all OFF!"

When Mommy saw herself in the mirror, she felt happy, more beautiful, and stronger than ever. She couldn't wait to go home and show Autumn!

When Mommy arrived, Autumn gave her the biggest
smile and exclaimed, "Mommy, I love your hair!
You have HAIR LIKE ME!"

"Thank you, honey! When I was at the hair salon, I saw all kinds of beautiful women with very different hairstyles."

"And you know what? All of those women had princess hair because princess hair can look different on everyone," Mommy said.

Mommy continued, "You are beautiful and your hair is, too. So I decided to style my hair like yours. Princesses are princesses because they are beautiful on the inside. They can have whatever hair they want!"

"Now, Autumn, repeat after me," Mommy said.

"SO I MUST HAVE PRINCESS HAIR!" Autumn shouted.

"Oh Mommy, I love you and I love my hair too. But, are you still a princess?" Autumn asked.
"Of course! We are both princesses with our princess hair."

Hey Parents, Teachers and Friends!

Now that you've read Hair Like Me with your little one, help them understand their true, natural beauty! I've provided a few questions to assist you with having meaningful dialogue with your child about self-image and beauty.

What is your favorite way to style your hair?

What is one thing that you love about yourself?

What is the most beautiful feature on your head, face, or body?

Think about someone you love or really like a lot. What is one thing that makes them special?

MEET HEATHER

Heather Burris is a public health professional and a
gifted writer. Hair Like Me is her first published project.
Heather also enjoys reading, traveling, and spending quality time with
her family and friends. She is a wife to Brad, and mother to Autumn and
BJ. Follow her at www.joifulthoughts.com or @joifulthoughts.

MEET ARIEL

Ariel Mendez is an author/illustrator with a public policy background.
She has a passion for children's literature and loves helping writers make
their books a reality. She lives in Montgomery County, MD with her
husband and sons. Follow her book making adventures at
www.arielmendez.com or @arielmwrites.

CPSIA information can be obtained
at www.ICGtesting.com
Printed in the USA
LVHW072129020519
616500LV00015B/505/P